Chapel-en-le-Frith
in old picture postcards volume 2

by Mike Smith

European Library ZALTBOMMEL/THE NETHERLANDS

GB ISBN 90 288 1401 9

© 1999 European Library – Zaltbommel/The Netherlands

No part of this book may be reproduced in any form, by print, photoprint, microfilm or any other means, without written permission from the publisher.

Introduction

Chapel-en-le-Frith is one of the Peak District's best-kept secrets. The main route from the Manchester conurbation now by-passes the settlement; few tourists visit Chapel and some of those who do are unaware of its fine Old Town, which is largely hidden behind the façades of the main street. Even the Market Place is raised above street level.

For those who do venture into the Market Place and the cobbled streets and alleyways which surround the parish church, there are very rich rewards. There is a profusion of monuments, including old stocks, ancient crosses, fascinating gravestones and other evocative memorials. On close inspection, the apparently simple gritstone buildings reveal surprising details, amongst which are stone mounting steps, a relief of a bull's head, eccentric door frame decorations, and name plates and date stones which give evidence of former use.

Chapel-en-le-Frith is also one of the Peak District's most neglected assets. In common with most small towns, Chapel has suffered shop closures, and there has also been some physical neglect of the fabric in the oldest areas, but there is now considerable cause for optimism. The town's Regeneration Committee has been re-formed and a partnership has been forged between the Parish, Borough and County Councils, the local traders and the Amenity Society. Physical improvements, such as street planters, hanging baskets, better road and pavement surfacing, improved street furniture, and new heritage boards, are gradually being put into place.

These are not the only alterations taking place in Chapel-en-le-Frith. In fact, the Millennium marks a time of unprecedented change for the town. A brand new Infants' School is being built; there is a rapid growth in new housing; traffic-calming measures have been introduced which have changed the configuration of the main road; the ninety year old Ferodo Company, whose name has been linked for so long with the name of the town, has become Federal Mogul; and the old market town has now become a supermarket town, with the construction of a new superstore at the heart of the settlement.

In her recently published book 'The Warming Stone', Ada Hitchens has charted Chapel life in the twentieth century. Life in the twenty-first century will be very different. But the Millennium is a time for looking back, as well as forward. Chapel-en-le-Frith has a history which spans 775 years. Since its origin as a settlement in the Royal Forest of the Peak, Chapel has been a market town, a staging post on cross-Pennine trade routes, and has played a major role in the development of transport. Tradition and pageantry have always had a strong hold in the town, and well-dressing, which was introduced just four years ago, has now become established as another annual event.

Within the boundaries of Chapel Parish, there are many picturesque hamlets, each with a unique history, there is an unusually high concentration of country houses in the district, and the surrounding scenery of high gritstone ridges is very fine indeed.

Volume 1 of 'Chapel-en-le-Frith in old picture postcards' contained photographs and picture postcards of Chapel and its Parish from the nineteenth century to 1930. This second volume uses some more recent pictures, including the superb photographs of F.B. Hills, and charts the great changes which have taken place.

I am greatly indebted to the many people who have helped me during the preparation of this book. Jean Bailey, the late Brian Bailey, Peter Helps, Rev. Nick Braylesford, Ian Green, Hilary Batterbee, Michael Hallam, Donna Kadzewska, Sheila Nadin, Graham Harper, the Federal Mogul Company, and the staff of Chapel Infants' School have all been kind enough to loan me photographs and postcards. Fr. Moynihan supplied information on the R.C. church; Bryan McGee kindly dug out information on Blackbrook; Graham Harper shared with me his considerable knowledge of the development of the Ferodo Company; Ada Hitchens allowed me to use the photographs of F.B. Hills and others from her collection, and shared her reminiscences with me; Donna Kadzewska gave me much valuable information; Bob Mulholland of Caron Publications kindly gave me permission to quote from 'The Warming Stone'; the staff at Images, Buxton, showed patience and care when producing laser copies of old prints; and the staff at Chapel-en-le-Frith and Buxton libraries were most helpful.

There are a number of books which contain information about the history of Chapel-en-le-Frith. Worthy of particular mention are: Henry Kirke's 'Chapel-en-le-Frith, Capital of the Peak'; William Bralesford Bunting's books on the Church of St. Thomas Becket and the town; Alan Watson's books on Chinley, Whitehough and Bugsworth; Ada Hitchens' 'The Warming Stone'; Marguerite Bellhouse's books on Combs; and Graham Harper's 'Brakes and Friction Materials'. Readers are also encouraged to seek information from the Hearse House Visitor Centre, to explore the many footpaths in the parish by using the Amenity Society's walkabout leaflets and to follow the Parish Council's 'Old Town Trail'.

The Millennium is a milestone in history and, particularly at a time of great change, an appropriate moment to take stock of what is still in place and what has gone before. Any errors in recording and interpreting the history of Chapel-en-le-Frith are solely my responsibility.

Mike Smith, 1999

1 This splendid photograph of Dane's Yard was taken half a century ago by F.B. Hills, an evacuee who came to live in Chapel-en-le-Frith. Dane's Yard marks the interface between the churchyard of St. Thomas Becket's and Chapel's fine Old Town. It is approached from Burrfields by a road which is flanked by a dozen stout trees, known locally as the Twelve Apostles. The Bull's Head Inn is located, in the very best English tradition, just outside the church gates. Solid gritstone houses line the street known as Market Place, which leads to the Market Place proper. This delightful scene is little changed to this day, although the Bull's Head no longer functions as an inn. However, the building does retain a set of stone mounting steps and an impressive relief of a bull's head set above an elaborate doorway, which is topped by a delicately fashioned fanlight.

2   Little, if anything, remains of the thirteenth century chapel which was built by the foresters of Bowden on a spur of land in the Royal Forest of the Peak, but the present church occupies the lofty site of the original chapel-of-ease, and the Parish Church of St. Thomas Becket symbolises 775 years of continuity in a town which is currently undergoing rapid change. The tower and south front owe their classical appearance to a remodelling carried out in 1733. The north face, shown here, has a more Gothic feel. Continuity is also represented at the Sexton's Hut, which is located at the south-east corner of the churchyard. A stone inscription reads: 'Peter Bramwell for 52 years sexton at the said church. His son 40. His grandson 38. His great grandson 50. His great great grandson 43. His great great great grandson 39. 1631-1893.'

Parish Church, Chapel-en-le-Frith.

3   The nave of the church is illuminated by a Flemish-style chandelier, acquired in 1731. The box pews, first installed in 1834, once featured brass name plates, but these were removed in 1894, for safe keeping in the vestry. The stained-glass tripartite window at the head of the north aisle was destroyed a few years ago when an out-building caught fire. Its replacement, which was designed by David Pilkington and Steven Parsonson, was dedicated by the Bishop of Ripon in 1997. The semi-abstract motifs on the new window are very colourful. Red areas represent fire; descending gold flashes, against a heavenly blue, symbolise spiritual food and drink; royal purple is used to represent the King of Kings; and the design features a background cross. Although the new window is uncompromisingly modern, its vertical grid is designed to match the structure of older stained-glass windows in the church.

4 This winter scene was taken from the head of Burrfields, the sloping land which runs immediately east of the churchyard. The background features in this photograph have barely changed over the years: the patchwork fields of Peaslows still form a backcloth to views of Town End; the Victorian houses on Hayfield Road, which runs across the centre of our picture, are little changed; and the tower of the Wesleyan Church still dominates the huddle of buildings at the eastern end of Market Street. But the foreground features have altered out of all recognition: a new housing estate has been developed at the head of Burrfields, and the little market town of Chapel has now become a supermarket town. The new store, which opened in 1998, stretches from the large edifice on the right, which once housed the Auxiliary Fire Service, to the left extremity of our picture; the supermarket car park completely covers the field below the hedgerow.

5   Church Brow, the steep, cobbled street which runs from the church to Market Street, is the most picturesque lane in town and one of the Peak District's best surprises. The walls of some of the cottages have been rendered since this photograph was taken, but their general contours are unaltered. The echelon roofline of the continuous terrace is particularly pleasing on the eye, and the peculiar doorpost decoration found on most of the houses is a characteristic feature of older dwellings in the town. Horizontally-placed stone slabs project from the head and foot of the stone doorframes. As little attempt was made to achieve symmetry when these stones were selected, the effect is highly eccentric, but charming. Church Brow bears a strong resemblance to Gold Hill, in Dorset, famous as the setting for a Hovis commercial.

Church Brow, Chapel en le Frith.

6   The people of Chapel have always loved a ceremony. The Market Place is the traditional setting for a number of annual pageants, such as the switching-on of the Christmas lights and, in more sombre vein, the November Remembrance Day commemoration. There is also a long tradition of a Market Place bonfire on Guy Fawkes Night. Ada Hitchens gives an evocative description of the scene in her book 'The Warming Stone': 'It was certainly a most exciting sight to see the flames and all the people and the Market Place in the glow of the fire. We knew that when we went home there would be homemade treacle toffee and parkin for us. It was a wonderful scene and, as the fire burned low, people put potatoes in the embers to roast.'

7 The Market Place was also the setting for a ceremony to mark the 700th Anniversary of the founding of St. Thomas Becket Church. The chapel-of-ease which had been erected by the foresters of the Royal Forest of the Peak was consecrated on 7th July 1225, the Feast Day of St. Thomas Becket, who had been murdered at Canterbury Cathedral in 1170. Eventually, the chapel gained independence from the mother church of St. Peter at Hope and became the parish church of the Capital of the Peak. The building has been much altered over the years, with major rebuildings in 1380, 1733 and 1890. The 700th Anniversary was marked by an ox-roast. Children took turns to rotate the spit and Rev. Norman Bennett cut the first slice.

8   When this photograph was taken, the Market Place occupied a more extensive area than it does today. Although some of the market area was raised above the level of Market Street, it seemed to be much more integral with the main road than it is now. This shot was taken in the early years of the century on Cattle Market Day. A large mural showing a cattle market in 1897 is on display in the Olde Stocks Café at the corner of the Market Place. Animals were brought to market on the first Thursday of each month and an annual Wool Fair was held on the nearest Tuesday to the Feast Day of St. Thomas. These events no longer take place, but the tradition of a weekly stall market, which was revived in 1978, continues to this day.

9 This photograph from the immediate post-war years shows a picturesque Market Place which is completely surfaced in cobbles and largely devoid of cars. Today, cobbles no longer extend into the roadway and parked cars litter the scene. The stocks and other Market Place monuments have now been set on a paved area which acts as a kind of dais and also enables the monuments to be quarantined from the traffic. The large gabled house at the far left of the photograph, which was known locally as the White House, was demolished in recent years to make way for a new Co-op. The Electricity Show Rooms are no longer housed in the arcaded building, but the glass-topped arcades have survived. The Roebuck Inn has new signs but its attractive fascia remains intact.

10　The Market Cross is clearly visible in this late nineteenth century photograph, but the central feature of the Market Place is a very fine lamp standard. The buildings are sturdy and perhaps a little dowdy, but they form a harmonious whole. The present-day post office is seen in its previous incarnation as the Swan Hotel, also known as the Swan with Two Necks, and the adjacent building has yet to acquire its arcade. Only a low wall separates Market Place from Market Street and there is no pavement between the two thoroughfares. Pedestrians walking up the main street are drawn naturally into the market area.

11 This later photograph of Market Place is dominated by the line of trees which have rather sealed off the market area from the main road. The Swan Inn has become the post office, although it carries to this day the inscription 'T.O.B. 1773'. Arcading has appeared on the north side of Market Place and a horse trough has been erected to mark Queen Victoria's Diamond Jubilee of 1897. Market Place was reduced in width in 1936, when the main road was widened to cope with increasing traffic. Ironically, the road was recently narrowed once again in a traffic-calming scheme which involved the chicaning of the main road by the construction of a series of 'pregnant pavements'.

12   Stocks were once commonplace in English towns and villages, and many survive in market places and village greens to this day. The practice of hurling abuse, rotten food and other unsavoury morsels at the pilloried victims was a popular sadistic sport. Chapel's stocks could well date from the Cromwellian period. They have been much renovated over the years and they now sit on a freshly cobbled dais. The stocks suffered damage as a result of a road accident involving a charabanc in 1920, but they are now isolated from passing vehicles and enjoy the protection of a chained perimeter.

13 Crosses are also a characteristic feature of English towns and villages. They were once used as a focus for open-air preaching, particularly at a time when trade took place alongside gatherings for worship. Chapel's Market Cross, which is much weathered, may possibly have an ecclesiastical origin. There is much dispute about its age. Some suggest the structure dates from the thirteenth century; others claim to have detected a date of 1636 on its surface. As a result of the road widening of 1936, the monument now stands up against the railings. When the alterations took place, it was found that the Cross stands on five steps. The fourth step is at the current ground level; the fifth step remains buried.

14   Beyond the market area, Market Street evolves into High Street. The solid, four-square buildings on the right of the road once housed the police superintendent and sergeant, and there were police cells here. The characteristic wall-mounted police station lamp is clearly visible in our photograph. Before the construction of High Street and further ribbon development along Manchester Road, this area was known as Town Head and was occupied by farms. Beyond the police station is the Old Parsonage. The plot on High Street was first acquired as a parsonage in 1720 and was used as an official residence by vicars of the parish until 1849.

15   The Poor Law Amendment Act of 1834 was designed to discourage the able-bodied poor from applying for Poor Relief. The Act stipulated that relief should only be given to those who entered a workhouse, where the quality of life was designed to be worse than that of the lowest paid labourer, in order to prevent 'idlers' from applying for free board and lodging. As time went by, conditions in Britain's workhouses began to improve and care became much more humane. Chapel's workhouse for a hundred paupers was established at the Elms in 1840. The site is now occupied by Eccles Fold, a new complex opened by the Duke of Edinburgh in 1984, which includes a modern sheltered housing scheme and a day care centre. Eccles Fold provides first-class support to the elderly.

16 Rev. George Hall, who was appointed Vicar of Chapel in 1836, campaigned for the provision of a new school, to improve the education of poorer children in the parish. The Church Boys' School was completed in 1839 on a site, on the south side of High Street, donated by Rev. William Bagshawe. The building, which is grade 2-listed, was designed by Robert Potter of Lichfield. It has a very impressive frontage, with a massive, two-storey, gabled central section, flanked by two single-storey wings. The façade has a picturesque array of mullioned and transomed windows. Girls' and Infants' School buildings were added in 1889, and the present Church of England Infants' School currently occupies all the buildings on this site, as well as the Horsa huts on the north side of the main road. Our picture shows former teachers at the Infants' School. Back row, left to right: Jean Garner, Sheila Finn, Mary Embury and Dorothy Bradley. Front row: Margaret Hawkins, Muriel Yates (Headteacher) and Mary Hadwin.

17 The daily crossing of the main road by Infants' School children is a hazard which has worried the parents and teachers of Chapel for many years. The Horsa huts, erected as 'temporary' structures half a century ago, have provided inadequate classrooms, and they have vibrated and suffered noise pollution each time a train has thundered along the railway line which runs close to the huts. After a long and vociferous campaign, a brand new school is now being provided for infants on a site adjacent to Warmbrook Junior School at Town End. The provision of a new school, which is scheduled to open in September 1999, is long overdue, but it is also to be hoped that a new lease of life can be found for the splendid Victorian buildings on the south side of High Street. Our photograph shows former pupils of Chapel Infants' School.

18   Many photographs exist of recruits leaving Chapel-en-le-Frith in September 1914. Our picture shows volunteers and their loved ones marching purposefully to Chapel's Central Station. 599 Chapel men served in the Great War; all their names are listed on the War Memorial in the Market Place, an unusual and generous tribute. Thirteen per cent of the men were killed; their names are marked on the memorial by crosses. Many Chapel families were deeply affected by the suffering and the death of men in the First World War. Those harrowing times have not been forgotten and they are brought to the fore in the annual Remembrance Day Parade along Market Street and the solemn ceremony which is held in the Market Place.

19 This photograph of a cheerful group camouflages the fact that news from the front became ever more grim as the war progressed. The pages of the Buxton Advertiser became increasingly occupied by news of fatalities. One soldier from Chapel, who was injured and taken to the Western General Hospital in Manchester, kept a journal in which he asked fellow patients to record their war experiences. One entry reads: 'After being at the front for just four months, I was unlucky enough to be badly wounded in the face. When the men came to pick up the wounded they passed me by, leaving me because they thought I wouldn't last very long. I was left there for twelve hours before being rescued.'

20   Sport, particularly in the form of bowls, football and cricket, has always played a big part in Chapel life. Chapel United Football Club was formed in 1946 from the amalgamation of the pre-war Albion and Corinthians clubs. Cricket is popular in all the local villages and many of the grounds, including that of Chapel Cricket club, occupy idyllic locations in the hills of the High Peak. Our photograph shows the Chapel Ladies' Cricket Team of 1942. This was the heyday of ladies' cricket in the town; Connie Pink, the captain (pictured here with bat in hand), was the star player of a very good team.

Marion Bagshawe of Ford Hall is the lady at the top right of the picture.

21 Swimming was also a popular activity for people in the area. An open-air swimming pool at Park Hall, near Hayfield, was much used by local people, and Roeside, in Chapel itself, also became the site for an open-air pool. Facilities at Roeside included dressing rooms and a tea room. Each July, the pool was the setting for the Chapel Swimming Club's annual gala, an event which attracted a large number of participants and spectators. Unfortunately, the pool could not meet modern hygiene standards and had to be closed. Although there are now indoor pools in nearby towns, 'Johnny Middleton's Pool' is much missed by the people of Chapel.

22 This view of Chapel-en-le-Frith from the Horderns shows the Old Town in its High Peak setting, at the heart of a vast bowl which is rimmed by a series of gritstone ridges. The church and the original settlement were built on a spur of land which runs eastwards from Eccles Pike, a conical hill which stands in isolation at the heart of the wide valley, like an antenna at the centre of a radio telescope. Writing in the nineteenth century, Britten and Bayley gave the following classic description of Chapel in their book 'Beauties of England and Wales': 'A small, but neat town, situated in the declivity of a convex hill, which rises in the midst of a spacious concave, formed by the mountains at the extremity of this county.'

23   Until 1937, the Roman Catholics of Chapel-en-le-Frith had no place of worship in the town; most attended services in Tideswell. Mr. and Mrs. Carter (known for Carter's Little Liver Pills) from the Hope Valley were the main benefactors who enabled the Church of St. John Fisher and St. Thomas More to be built on Horderns Road. The church, which was blessed by the Bishop of Nottingham on 1st October 1937, is a small, neat building constructed in stone, including a few pieces of the beautiful, pink Crist Quarry stone which also adorns some parts of the parish church. The church was designed by A. Lowcock of Bakewell, and built by Green and Son, a local builder. The exterior has traditional elements, but also touches of the Modernist styling of the period. Fr. Cafferky of Tideswell, who was also given charge of the Chapel church, spent two years making a carved oak altar for the new building. Other carvings were produced by the Huntstone brothers of Tideswell.

24 Chapel-en-le-Frith has an unusually high concentration of country houses, a legacy of the Royal Forest of the Peak, when 'burgages' were granted in exchange for services to the Crown. Bradshaw Hall, on the lower slopes of Eccles Pike, is one of Chapel's oldest and most beautiful houses. The interior has a moulded cornice and a frieze wth the legend: 'A man without mercy of mercy shall miss but he shall have mercy that merciful is: Love God but not Gould.' The old hall has a particularly grand Jacobean gateway, constructed in 1620. The semi-circular entrance arch is flanked by fluted, shouldered pilasters and topped by a stepped, moulded cornice, which bears the coat-of-arms of Francis Bradshawe, cousin of Judge John Bradshawe, who presided at the trial of King Charles 1.

25 The present Bank Hall, which was built in the nineteenth century, occupies a superb site on the slopes of Combs Moss. The south front of the house has large bay windows and a prominent, elaborate stone balcony above the main entrance; the Venetian doorcase has floral motifs and is flanked by columns. The bay window in the dining room retains its fine botanical painted glass, but the panel paintings, by Caldecott and Armstrong, which once decorated this fine room, were sold some years ago to an American buyer. Like Bradshaw Hall, Bank Hall has a splendid gateway, probably designed by W.E. Nesfield, who was responsible for much of the interior. In addition, there is a superb lodge, which has high gables, timber framing, timber studwork and terracotta tiles. The massive, furrowed and corbelled brick chimney stack is particularly elaborate. Bank Hall Lodge is the former home of the architect Raymond Unwin.

26   The story of Nanny's Well is told on the plaque which was placed here in 1998: 'According to tradition, all medicinal springs are under the protection of a guardian spirit. This particular well may have been under the protection of St. Anne or St. Ninnian, names which became corrupted to 'Nanny's.' A survey carried out in 1895 reported that the water which emanates here comes from a spring of considerable depth and that in some respects the water of this well is of the same nature as that from the Tunbridge Wells springs. The land around the well was given to Chapel-en-le-Frith Parish Council by Mrs. Hannah Timms on 17th August 1904'. To date, there has been no well-dressing at Nanny's Well, but this ancient Derbyshire custom was introduced to Chapel as an annual event by the town's Amenity Society in 1995. The number of dressings displayed during the first week in July has now risen to four, and the addition of a fifth dressing at this ancient spring is under consideration.

27   The Amenity Society also has plans, in association with the National Trust and the Parish Council, to erect a toposcope on the summit of Eccles Pike. The toposcope would identify the Dark Peak hills which are visible in the superb 360-degree panorama which can be seen from the summit of this prominent peak, located just 1.5 miles from the centre of Chapel-en-le-Frith. Chinley Churn, Cracken edge, Mount Famine and South Head form the northern horizon, and the great ridge of Combs Moss dominates the view to the south. The Kinder Scout plateau, which contains the highest land in the Peak District, is visible to the north-east. The glistening waters of Combs Reservoir are the predominant feature in the valley to the south, and the villages of Whitehough and Chinley occupy the valley to the north. Six acres of land on the summit of Eccles Pike were given to the National Trust by Mrs. Spencer of Frith Knoll, as a contribution to King George VI's Coronation celebrations.

28   Combs Lake, covering some 80 acres of the valley which runs west of Chapel-en-le-Frith, was constructed in 1794 to service the Peak Forest Canal. The sheet of water, which is surrounded by the hills of the Dark Peak, is highly picturesque, although the sender of this card noted that the lake had almost dried up after a period of drought. The village of Combs, at the south-eastern corner of the lake, has the Beehive Inn as its focus. The present inn was built in 1863 from profits made from the Irish 'navvies' who constructed the nearby railway line. According to Mrs. Bellhouse, historian of Combs, the old Beehive stood on the former road to Chapel via Dane Hey and Combs Meadows, sideways to its present position on the village green. The 'Green', which is now tarmacked, really was a green before the Great War. There is much dispute about the pronunciation of the village place-name. Locals prefer 'Combs'; incomers tend to favour 'Coombs'.

29   This superb view of Chapel-en-le-Frith was taken from South Station, now the only remaining station in the town. The tower of St. Thomas Becket Church dominates the Old Town, a huddle of buildings which have South Head and Mount Famine as a backdrop. The later ribbon development on Manchester Road can be seen on the left of the picture. Chapel is now a commuter town for the Manchester conurbation and the scene of a great deal of new house building. The population of Chapel Parish in 1931 was 5,662; it is now over 8,000, and rising. Much of the green foreground in this photograph is now occupied by a large housing estate, unfortunately constructed in brick. The time cannot be far away when housing developments will reach as far as the railway line.

30   Whitehough is a picturesque hamlet situated 1.25 miles north-west of Chapel, in the Blackbrook Valley, and at the foot of Chinley Churn. The settlement is centred around Whitehough Old Hall, a very attractive, late Elizabethan manor house. In 1806, the Whitehough Estate was sold off as lots and a paper mill was built on part of the land. The original owners of the mill lived at Whitehall, the large house shown here. Lord Molson, who was Member of Parliament for the High Peak from 1939 to 1960, lived here in the Fifties. The stretch of water in the foreground is a dam which was built for the paper mill. The Chapel by-pass, completed in 1987, runs close by the hamlet, but Whitehough has managed to retain its quiet village atmosphere.

31 The waterfall at Whitehough was created in 1833 to provide water power for the paper mill. The course of Black Brook was altered and three dams were constructed. In 1874, the Whitehall Works were converted into a factory for bleaching and dyeing textiles. In 1924, Dr. Babbington, an Austrian chemist who owned the works at the time, replaced steam power with electricity. Bernard Wardles, the silk and cloth printing business, moved into the Whitehall works at the beginning of the Second World War, when their Bridgnorth factory was commandeered by the Air Ministry. The track of the High Peak Tramway, constructed in 1796 to bring limestone from the quarries at Dove Holes to the Peak Forest Canal, runs through Whitehough.

32 The long tradition of an annual carnival was revived in 1970 after some years' lapse. Our photograph shows the Crowning of the 1938 Carnival Queen, Iris Harrison, by the 1937 Queen, Donna Heather. Iris' attendants, on the right, include Betty Ruhorn and Lorna Warhurst; Donna's attendants, on the left, include Marian Ramsey, May Fletcher and Carina Weaver. According to tradition, the Crowning of the Chapel Carnival Queen was followed by the arrival of the Cotton Queen, who was sponsored by the Daily Dispatch and the Whitworth Doubling Company. In these pre-war days, the crowning ceremony took place on the football field on Park Road, an area which is now covered by housing; the Master of Ceremonies was Cmdr. Cook. Donna Heather remembers that there was heavy rain on both the 1937 and 1938 Carnival days; the Queens and their retinues were very muddy by the time they left the football field and much scrubbing was needed before the traditional Carnival Evening Dance at the Town Hall.

33   Since the war, Carnival events have taken place in the Memorial Park. As our photograph shows, the park occupies an idyllic position, in a natural bowl of the Dark Peak. The War Memorial Park was opened in 1921, four years after the opening of the Needham Recreation Ground on Ashbourne Lane. The entrance gate to the park is particularly impressive and was featured on the first Amenity Society well-dressing in 1995 (dried rhubarb leaves were used to represent the stonework). Chapel-en-le-Frith's parks are much valued assets, but the activities which take place in them have changed greatly over the years. Since the war, fashions have moved from tennis to skateboarding to rollerblading. The town's bands have often performed there, although there was much dispute in 1922 about the playing of music in the Memorial Park on Sundays. The Parish Council is to add a Perfumed Garden to the park as part of its Millennium projects.

34 As Chapel-en-le-Frith is situated over 700 ft above sea-level, it is subject to extreme weather conditions at the best of times. But few winters can rival that of 1947 when Market Street was well and truly covered in snow for long periods. In fact, there was snow on the ground for some seventy days, and public and private transport was severely disrupted. One locomotive became marooned in a huge snowdrift at Dove Holes and some passengers had to spend the entire night on the train. In the Cowburn railway tunnel workmen laboured for twelve hours to remove icicles, some of which were 20 ft long and 3 ft thick. In his entertaining little book 'Arctic Buxton', Stuart Whatley relates the experiences of Freda Mottershead, who lived in New Mills, but worked in the Ferodo factory at Chapel-en-le-Frith. Freda remembers walking to the factory with her colleagues in a blizzard which blanked out all landmarks and froze her eyelashes to her cheek.

35 Ada Hitchens, pictured here, appears to be rather enjoying the winter of 1947. Ada, now 89 years old, is the author of 'The Warming Stone', a reminiscence of her childhood in Chapel, in which she recalls a way of life which vanished long ago. Ada describes the drudgery of housework and the slavery of washday in the days before labour-saving devices; the ever present threat of disease and the application of homemade remedies. For example, children with whooping cough were held over hot lime kilns! Life was hard, but people were proud, dignified and resourceful: everyone baked their own bread and Ada's mother made delicious nettle beer; pavements were swilled and steps scoured in a weekly ritual; the stationmaster touched his cap to passengers; and children obtained simple pleasures from marbles, hoops and conkers. Ada's book charts a revolution in domestic and working life, including the coming of electricity and the motor car and the decline of the working horse.

36 This view of Market Place shows the Cross, the War Memorial and the King's Arms. The gritstone Market Cross is eighteen feet high and scheduled as an ancient monument. Kelly's Directory of 1904 dates the structure as 1643. The War Memorial, a grade 2-listed monument, carries the inscription 'Erected in 1919 to record the honoured names of men from the Parish of Chapel-en-le-Frith who served in the Great War'. The panels which list the names of the town's soldiers are framed by four distinctive, curved and stepped buttresses, topped by acanthus leaf brackets. The King's Arms was once known as Town Head and consisted of two farm houses, Old House Farm and New House Farm. The façade which is visible here has been retained on the present inn, but the walls are now covered with a coat of whitewash. The building used to have an entrance which opened directly on to High Street, but this has been blocked up. The King's Arms is just one of four inns on the perimeter of Market Place. There were even more in former times.

37 The large number of inns in the vicinity of Market Place is testimony to Chapel's long history as a staging post on trade and transport routes across the Pennines. The Royal Oak, shown here, was a departure point for the Peak Ranger and the Celerity, stage coaches which ran to Stockport and Manchester. The inn also housed the Magistrates' Court. The Royal Bank of Scotland building, which can be glimpsed to the right of the Royal Oak, is the former Pack Horse Inn; the Dog Inn is immediately right of the bank. The low building with its gable end fronting the main road was once used to house a taxi. Its demolition left an untidy gap in the streetscape of the Conservation Area which remains to this day. The Chapel Regeneration Committee is anxious to fill this space as soon as possible. The half-timbered building on the left of the junction now houses the Vecchia Italia restaurant, one of Chapel's greatest assets.

38 This photograph from half a century ago shows a quiet main street in a pleasant country town. There are no road markings, cars are few and far between and the person who is pushing a cycle up the street is not afraid to use the carriageway. As car ownership became universal, traffic volumes on the main road increased alarmingly. The Chapel by-pass, opened in 1987, reduced the flow of north-south traffic through the town, but did little to reduce the east-west flow. Vehicle speeds, exacerbated by the length and steepness of the main road, also presented a major hazard. Traffic-calming measures, including pavement projections and mini-roundabouts, have helped to manage the traffic and reduce speeds, but they also disfigure the street scene. However, pavement planters, introduced by the traders and the Parish Council, have helped to soften their impact. Unfortunately, the pavement flagstones, clearly visible here, were replaced some years ago by tarmac.

39 As several haulage firms are based in Chapel-en-le-Frith, heavily-laden vehicles pass frequently up and down the main street. Congestion is now a major problem, but pedestrians and other road users are at least secure in the knowledge that modern vehicles have efficient braking systems. This 1933 accident illustrates past hazards. A runaway steam lorry, laden with stone, has crashed into the Old Brewery. In a yet earlier age, it was the 'untidy and ragged brakes' on wagons which he saw negotiating the steep hills of the High Peak that inspired Herbert Frood of Combs to develop his new braking material. Frood's brake linings came to be used on trains as well as road vehicles. The impact of the railways on the High Peak was a cause of great concern to Henry Kirke, who wrote: 'The shriek of the locomotive has banished all romance, and rudely destroyed the seclusion of these remote valleys and hills, and they have become as the rest of the world.'

40 There is no sign of cars or lorries in this view of Market Street. Two riders are happy to take their horses down the middle of the carriageway and the children who are taking a ride on the milk float have no worries about their safety. The house in the foreground, formerly a hairdressers, has now lost both its shop window and its front door, but there have been almost no other alterations to the contours and façades of the solid stone buildings which line the northern side of Market Street. Sadly, all the trees in this picture have now disappeared. The large tree at the foot of the road has been replaced by the forecourt of a petrol filling station, which has a huge canopy, incongruous in both material and scale. The round-headed window on the left of the picture belongs to the Primitive Methodist Church. The neat, symmetrical façade of the building, which now houses John Kelly's joinery business, has been well cared for by the present owners.

41   Our picture shows the Primitive Methodist Centenary Sunday School, on the south side of Market Street. An inscription on a stone slab set into the wall of the building indicates that the school was constructed in 1910. The Primitive Methodist Bethel, glimpsed in our previous photograph, was built in 1852. Primitive Methodism had a considerable following in the High Peak area; its origins were in Burslem and the first camp meeting of the breakaway movement was held at the beginning of the nineteenth century on Mow Cop, near Stoke-on-Trent. Bunting lists Thomas Potts, Thomas Shepley and John Walton as local pioneers of Primitive Methodism. The Market Street façade of the Sunday School has been drastically altered and the building is now used as a tyre services depot. Huge tyres for heavy goods vehicles now occupy the land in the foreground of our photograph.

42 The dark stone and the tall lancet windows of Chapel's Town Hall give the building a church-like appearance. Its style is perhaps best described as 'Austere Gothic'. The Town Hall was erected in 1850 at the expense of Dr. Slacke of Bowden Hall. The centenary celebrations, which took place in October 1950, included Olde Tyme Variety, a whist drive, three one-act plays and a Grand Concert featuring the Town Band and Chapel Male Voice Choir. The Magistrates held their courts here from 1850 until 1928, and the building also housed the Trustee Savings Bank, the Penny Bank and the High Peak Lodge of the Freemasons. The New Sessions House, as it was originally called, was acquired by the Council in 1928 and now houses the Parish Office and a branch of the County Library. Throughout its history, the Town Hall has provided a venue for the use of local organisations. Chapel Parish Council celebrated its centenary in 1994.

43 The building with the porthole-like upper window is the Hearse House of 1818. A large archway frames the room which once housed the Parish Hearse, available for hire to anyone who could provide a horse. The names of the Minister of the Parish in 1818 and his churchwardens are engraved on a stone plaque below the round window. The Hearse House was restored by Chapel-en-le-Frith Amenity Society and opened as a Visitor Centre by the Duchess of Devonshire in 1992. The centre houses exhibitions and has a display of artifacts, as well as a comprehensive selection of tourist information about the town and the surrounding district. The Amenity Society organises talks and local walks, coordinates well-dressing in the town, produces walking trails and gives Gold Awards in recognition of good local building design and environmental improvements.

44 When this photograph was taken, the Park Road area, immediately south of Market street and north of the Eaves Estates, was largely farmland, apart from a few large, red-brick villas and a tennis court belonging to the Ferodo company. The Target Wall, where the Volunteer Reserve and the 6th Battalion of the Sherwood Foresters practised shooting, was also in this vicinity. Ada Hitchens remembers the Target Field as 'a treasure house of wild flowers and grasses'. The Target Wall has been dismantled now, the road of limestone aggregate shown here has been tarmacked and the farmland has been replaced by an estate of Council houses. Local authority house building began about fifty years ago in the Park Road area and then extended to Thornbrook Road. Later developments in this area include a Health Centre and the Fire Station.

45 This charming photograph of Old Chapel was taken from Park Road shortly after the Second World War. The tower of St. Thomas Becket Church, which dominates this particular view and most views of Chapel from the surrounding hills, is largely an eighteenth century refashioning carried out by Platt of Rotherham. The 'new clothes', as Pevsner calls them, which were added by Platt, include obelisk pinnacles and a parapet. They give the tower a distinctive profile. The belfry contains six bells, five of which were cast at Gloucester by Abraham Rudhall. The tradition of ringing the Special Bells, such as the 8 p.m. Curfew Bell, the Apprentice Bell to signal the Shrove Tuesday half-day holiday, and the Passing Bells rung at funerals, stopped during the Second World War and was never revived.

46 Tom Longson's hay wagon dominates this view of Market Street, but the photograph is really an eloquent essay about a changing way of life. Ada Hitchens claims that this was the last hay cart to go through the streets of Chapel. Lorries and cars had largely taken over from horse-drawn vehicles when this photograph was taken and there are early signs here of the congestion which has become such a feature of the main street. Tom Longson, of Park Farm, and Walter Barlow, of Down Lee Farm, used to make door-to-door deliveries of milk throughout Chapel from their horse-drawn floats. Milkmen are still a feature of Chapel life and it is to be hoped that the service they provide is not destined to be a thing of the past. The boy on the float is Tom Longson's nephew Colin; the two gables on the right belong to the Primitive Methodist Bethel and the Hearse House.

47 This photograph also tells the story of change. The tree and wall on the right have both now disappeared. They mark the junction of Thornbrook Road and Market Street, where there is now a parade of shops. When Violet Carson (Ena Sharples of Coronation Street) came to open the new units, local people who were familiar with Ena's famous hairnet, were surprised by Violet's coiffured appearance. The trees on the left have been replaced by the entrance to the new supermarket and its petrol filling station. The incongruous white building just beyond the shop blind is the Empress Cinema. The picture house was managed by Eldred Fetcher, and Sarah Wildgoose played musical accompaniments to the silent films in a particularly flamboyant style. When the talkies were first shown here in March 1930, there was much excitement in the town. In the heyday of cinema-going there were three different programmes each week on show at the Empress. After its demise as a cinema, and before its sad demolition, the building was used as a bingo hall for a short time.

Market Street, Chapel-en-le-Frith.

48 There is a strong tradition of Methodism in Chapel-en-le-Frith. John Wesley made four visits to the town between 1740 and 1786. In 1748, Wesley proposed to Grace Murray, who had helped to nurse him back to health in Newcastle. Grace joined Wesley on his travels and the two were inseparable for five months. The pair even underwent a form of marriage ceremony in Ireland, but Charles Wesley objected to the liaison, and Grace married John Bennet, one of Wesley's leading preachers and his rival in love, whom she had also nursed at Newcastle. When John Bennet died at the age of 45, Grace moved to Chapel-en-le-Frith, where she lived until her death, at the age of 85, in 1803. A Wesleyan Chapel was first built at Town End in 1780. This was replaced in 1874 by the present building, which retains the date stone of the original chapel over its rear door. The recent extension to the front of the building is an excellent example of modern design which blends with the original lines.

WESLEYAN CHURCH, CHAPEL-EN-LE-FRITH

49 The Wesleyan Chapel has a spacious interior. The stained glass windows, erected in 1890, include memorial windows to members of the Smith, Sidebotham, Heathcott and Warhurst families. The fixed pews shown here have now been removed and replaced by wooden chairs which can be arranged as required. Further flexibility has been provided by the addition of a coffee bar and meeting room in the modern extension. During an evening service in the great freeze-up of 1929, all the lights inside the church went out just as Rev. Sidney Gordon announced the hymn 'Lead, Kindly Light'. The Buxton Advertiser reported that oil lamps had to be found before the singing could begin. This incident pales into insignificance when compared with the problems at Chinley Independent Chapel, where two hot water pipes burst and sprayed the congregation. When the caretaker went down to the boiler room to investigate he was overcome by fumes and rendered unconscious.

50 A Sunday School was established by Chapel Wesleyans during the eighteenth century. Bunting claims that the town's Methodists were actually pioneers of the Sunday School movement which was initiated by Robert Raikes. The first school meetings were held in cellars at Town End, one of which was quite dark and dingy. Later meetings took place in a specially constructed room on the north side of Market Street. This building was eventually converted into cottages, but the area is still known as Old School Yard. New School Rooms, originally constructed simply to house the Sunday School, were erected in 1853 on a site adjacent to the old chapel.

51 The Wesleyan School functioned solely as a Sunday School until 1870, when a day school was opened. The School Rooms were enlarged in 1887 and again in 1927. Our photograph shows the class of 1937 at Town End Methodists. The teacher is Mrs. Helps and the headmaster is Mr. Tuberfield. Many of the pupils shown here are still resident in Chapel. The present Chapel Junior School occupies a site at Warmbrook, just south of the Methodist Church, and the long-awaited new Infants' School is due to open in brand-new premises on adjacent land in September 1999. The Wesleyan School Rooms have now been converted into housing units in an imaginative scheme which retains the architectural integrity of the original building.

52 Town End, the cluster of stone-built houses and shops at the eastern extremity of Market Street and the foot of Buxton Road, has the feel and appearance of a separate village. The physical division between the centre of Chapel and Town End has become even more pronounced since the building of a large filling station and, more recently, the construction of the supermarket at the junction between the two communities. The solid, unpretentious properties shown here are typical Chapel houses. In the words of Henry Kirke, author of 'Chapel-en-le-Frith, Capital of the Peak': 'The houses have been substantially erected, but, it must be confessed, more with an eye to comfort than elegance.' A group of cottages on the right carries a distinct list, but this has not prevented their survival, complete with list, to the present day.

53 This much busier, celebratory scene at Town End took place at the head of Hayfield Road East. Chapel folk will recognise a number of local people, amongst whom are Martin and Agnes Kelly and Fred and Ada Heather. Many will also remember the busy Town End shops, such as Cluett's, who announced 'Cheese and bacon our speciality; service and civility our motto'; Barton's, who served ham, bacon, cheese and potted meat, delivered daily; Jimmy Featherstone's, later John Roe's, the newsagents, with its All Year Round Club to help people buy Christmas and birthday presents by instalments; Johnson's Sweet Shop, source of Lyon's Pola Maid Ice Creams; Cliff Johnson's Supper Bar, where customers could enjoy fish, chips, peas and tripe; and Bullock's Supper Bar, whose advertisement read 'When you've been to the cinema complete the evening with a delicious supper'.

54 The Town End section of Hayfield Road is a late nineteenth-century development, and its bay-windowed Victorian façades have survived largely unaltered, but the area beyond these dwellings is now undergoing enormous changes. The Hayfield Road Gasworks, shown here, closed before the Second World War. The land in this vicinity has been occupied by Hill's Garage and, more recently, Dave Ashton's Garage, but has now been cleared for the construction of a large new estate of private houses, built by a national building firm. The higher land is already covered by the Danesway Estate. In fact, Burrfields, the large area of sloping fields stretching from Hayfield Road up to the Parish Church, will soon be completely covered by a swathe of stone-faced private houses. The terrace of cottages in our picture, now known as Poplar Terrace, but formerly known as Pump Row, will survive alongside the new buildings.

55   Carnival floats are also a thing of the past on Hayfield Road. This superb streamlined float dates from an era when the Carnival Procession took a long route from Hayfield Road to Cockyard, and then on to the presentation arena; the current processional route by-passes Hayfield Road. The 'Hazel Grove Twins', Mr. Rowbotham and Mr. Clough, were once a regular feature of the procession; over the years, they managed to amass over £11,000 in their collection boxes. There is still keen competition for the prizes given by the Carnival Committee for best fancy dress and best decorated pubs, shops and houses. In the 1937 Carnival Week, Hardware Services, which continues as a thriving business to this day, was offering a prize of one guinea to anyone who could name and give the function of 100 items in their shop window.

56 Louis Pasteur once said: 'Chance favours the prepared mind.' Herbert Frood was born in 1864 at Balby, Yorkshire, but was a resident of Combs, near Chapel-en-le-Frith, when he set to work in his garden shed to assess the efficiency of various types of friction material on a water-driven dynamometer. One day, he chanced upon some stiff and oil-soaked belts which had been discarded at his father-in-law's Rossendale Belting Company. Back in his shed at Combs, Frood found that the material had excellent friction properties. From this chance discovery, he developed the revolutionary idea of using oil-impregnated woven cotton as a braking material. Our picture – courtesy of Ferodo Ltd and Federal Mogul – is a photographic reconstruction of Frood's house and his 'laboratory' at Combs.

57 Herbert Frood is seen here with his daughters at a 1906 gymkhana in the town. The Ferodo name, associated throughout the century with Chapel-en-le-Frith, is an anagram of the inventor's own surname and the initial of his wife, Elizabeth's Christian name. Frood used his 6hp Mercedes as a test bed for the development of his friction braking materials. His first brake blocks were used on horse-drawn vehicles, but they were then developed for use on motor buses, cars and locomotives. Frood's cotton-based friction material enabled the London omnibuses to satisfy the Police's requirement that they should be able to pull up in 14 ft from a speed of 12 mph. The pioneer's shed is now preserved in the grounds of the Hayfield Road factory, which has been a major source of employment for Chapel people for the last ninety years.

58 Frood began manufacturing his brake blocks at Gorton, Manchester, in 1897. Initially, coach builders were somewhat reluctant to use the new brakes but, once they became accepted, demand escalated rapidly. In 1902, Frood bought two old cotton mills in Chapel-en-le-Frith and set up his brake-lining factory there. In his advertisements, Frood compared his superior brake blocks to the old rope which 'requires many nails to hold in position' and, after slight wear, 'becomes ragged and soon wears away'. The London Omnibus Company were certainly convinced: they ordered Ferodo brakes for their 5,000 horse-drawn buses. Commissions followed for the new motor buses. The twin chimneys of the works, erected in 1925 and 1951, no longer pierce the Chapel skyline; they have now been dismantled.

59   The Ferodo Laboratory Block, on Hayfield Road, was opened by the Duke of Edinburgh in 1958. Its design bears some similarity to the famous Hoover Building in West London, in that a long, low façade is cleverly counterbalanced by strong vertical elements in the form of the mullions which subdivide the large window area. Interestingly, this postcard view has been slightly doctored: a pylon behind the building on the left has been brushed out and converted into a tree. The little factory gatehouse, which is out of shot, is also an architectural gem with its double-decked bay windows topped by a projecting canopy. Its style is strikingly similar to London Underground architecture. The Ferodo era, which has lasted for a century, is at an end. The Laboratory Block now bears the name 'Federal Mogul'.

60 Bowden Lane, at the eastern end of the town, has a rural and cosy atmosphere. Its varied, but harmonious assortment of cottages straggles a narrow, winding lane. The peace is broken by the busy by-pass link road which intersects Bowden Lane, but tranquillity is restored as the lane continues its journey to Chapel Milton via a pretty stretch of lane known as the Drum and Monkey. The origin of the name is something of a mystery. There is no evidence of the existence of a pub of this title in the area. The name may stem from the days when a pedlar visited the area with his drum and monkey.

61 The rural theme continues at the Wash, one of a number of pretty hamlets situated close to Chapel-en-le-Frith. The apparently haphazard scattering of cottages is little changed to this day. The attractive place-name may simply mean a watering place, or it could indicate a place where clothes, sheep or ore were washed. The stream which meanders so picturesquely through the hamlet tumbles down from the highest region of the Peak District on Kinder Scout. The prominent building at the head of the village was a Quaker Meeting House.

62   The first of the two great viaducts at Chapel Milton was constructed in 1866, the second in 1894. These twin structures are very impressive legacies of the Railway Age. The high-level roadbridge, which now crosses the road just south of the hamlet, is a monument to the Automobile Age; it carries the Chapel-Whaley Bridge by-pass, completed in 1987, across the Blackbrook Valley. A mill was established at Chapel Milton in 1391 for processing corn, and a rag mill operated here until 1946. The mill is in the middle of our photograph, under the central arches of the curved viaduct. There was a mill pond in front of the building. When John Wesley preached at this spot in 1745, his oratory was famously in competition with the sound of rushing water which had been released by the miller. Wesley claimed that his voice won the competition.

63 The bridge at New Smithy was built as part of a scheme to extend the Midland Railway to New Mills. The coming of the railway caused many changes in the little hamlet. The Turnpike, which ran in front of the Crown and Mytre, had to be diverted, and the village school had to be dismantled and rebuilt at Four Lane Ends. Ralph Harrison founded a Sunday School here in 1833, initially in the upper room of a barn and later in a permanent structure which evolved into a day school in 1858. Harrison was a great benefactor, giving bursaries to the children whose parents could not afford the school fees of a few pence a week. The Harrison family lived at Ainsworth Cottages, behind the Crown and Mytre. At the beginning of this century, this range of buildings became a holiday home for poor Jewish children. Joseph Ambrose Cooke, who owned the garage just beyond the bridge, had his own band and was musical director of Chapel Town Band. His garage provided cars and caravans for holidaymakers.

64 This superb photograph by F.B. Hills shows the Turnpike as it leaves New Smithy for its journey over the hills to Glossop. The building on the hill is White Knowle Methodist Chapel, founded in 1809 as a place of worship for farmers from the scattered farmsteads in the area. Sunday services were held at 4 p.m. for the convenience of the farming fraternity. A fire in 1978 put a temporary halt to services, but the little chapel was fully restored. The road rises to Peep O'Day, where there is a house with an eye-shaped window in its east wall. Legend has it that the window was designed so that the rising sun would wake the inhabitants of the bedroom. This area is surrounded by prominent High Peak summits: Chinley Churn and Cracken Edge to the west; South Head and Mount Famine to the east.

65 South Head is the shapely peak which can be seen through the railway bridge at New Smithy. This panoramic view shows South Head from Fox Holes. The hill, whose summit is 1622 ft above sea level, is the south-western bulwark of Kinder Scout, the great plateau which forms the roof of the Dark Peak. Bitter battles were fought here in the Thirties between ramblers and landowners. In the dark days of the Depression, walkers seeking release from the grimy northern industrial cities on the rim of the Peak District went to great lengths to assert their 'right to roam' on the privately owned grouse moors of Kinder. The ensuing battle resulted in imprisonment for some ramblers, but helped bring about access rights and, twenty years later, the establishment of the Peak District as Britain's first National Park.

66 The Chapel-en-le-Frith area has an unusually high concentration of country houses. Bowden Hall is situated in the hills to the east of the town. The present gritstone ashlar, Tudor Gothic style mansion was built in 1844 by Richard Lane of Manchester, but the estate is an ancient one. According to Bunting, the Bowdens originated in Bowdon, Cheshire, and were a leading Chapel family by the seventeenth century. Dr. Slacke, of Slack Hall, owned the Bowden Hall estates for a time in the nineteenth century. The stable block, not shown here, has a bellcote set on four wooden posts and a clockface just below the eaves. Mrs. Mary Bagshawe of nearby Ford Hall left money in her will for the founding of a little school at Bowden Head. The school operated until 1927. A path runs from Bowden Hall to the Parish Church.

67   Slack Hall stands almost in the path of Castleton Road. The hall, which dates from 1727, has a very attractive south front with twin gables, tiny blind oval windows in the gables, four twin-light mullions on each bay, and a deep central two-storey niche. When the Sheffield Turnpike was constructed, the new road split the garden of Slack Hall in two. The owners then constructed a new hall in the hollow to the south of Castleton Road. The Lingards, who were once residents here, were devout Quakers. Members of their family are buried in the Quaker Burial Ground in what is now the grounds of the Chestnut Centre, an otter and owl sanctuary which is one of the main tourist attractions of the area.

68 Ford Hall, the ancestral home of the Bagshawes, occupies a superb location, in a deep hollow below South Head. The house is a grand mixture of styles, but no less attractive for that. The present building probably dates from the seventeenth century, but a five-bay Georgian range was added in 1727 and a Gothic south front was built in 1845. There are also twentieth-century additions. Ford Hall will always be associated with William Bagshawe, Apostle of the Peak. He held secret non-conformist services at the hall after being expelled from his Ministry at Glossop, for refusing to conform to the Book of Common Prayer. Some clandestine services were held in a remote barn at Malcoff, provided by his mother-in-law.

69   The stream known as Black Brook runs down from the hills through the tiny hamlet of Blackbrook and then goes on to form the wide Blackbrook Valley that divides Eccles Pike from Chinley Churn. The waters of the brook were once used to feed a series of mills which were sited further downstream, and there was once a mill in the hamlet itself. Blackbrook has retained the atmosphere of a quiet little backwater, despite the proximity of the Chapel-Whaley Bridge by-pass, constructed in 1987. The hamlet was in the ownership of the Partington family from 1740 until this century, but the estates were sold off in lots from the Thirties onwards. The new by-pass may well disturb the peace of Blackbrook, but motorists using the road to enter the Peak District from the Manchester conurbation are able to enjoy a magnificent first view of the Dark Peak hills.

70 The little cul-de-sac hamlet of Bagshaw, which was first documented as Baggessawes in 1251, sits in the High Peak hills as easily and deferentially as a rock outcrop. The Peak Planning Board's survey of the village contains some lyrical descriptions. The report describes how Bagshaw 'sits within the landscape, following the fall of land along its length, with individual buildings set either side of a sinuous road', and points out that the ancient enclosure walls form a 'strong visual link with the surrounding landscape', which 'cocoons the settlement on all sides'. Bagshaw is a twentieth-century rarity: there has been almost no structural development in the village since the turn of the century; there are no shops; there is no pub, no street lighting, no road markings or street furniture, and no formal parking places.

71 The little Methodist Church at Bagshaw was built in 1833, to serve a large High Peak farming community. The farms retain their ancient enclosures, with an irregular pattern which stems from earlier medieval cultivation in the area. The village is linear and its one and only street follows a steep incline, with no through road beyond Bagshaw Hall Farm, at the head of the settlement. Most of the gritstone houses and farm buildings date from the eighteenth and nineteenth centuries. Many have attractive names, such as Peartree Cottage, Appletree Cottage, Rose Cottage, Ivy Cottage and Hawthorn Cottage. The gritstone building material and the simple, unsophisticated architecture blend superbly with the Dark Peak landscape, where almost the only colours are dull green and dark grey.

72 Buxton Road is now the link road from the by-pass into the town of Chapel-en-le-Frith. The wall on the left marks the point at which the High Peak Tramway crossed the road. The tramway was opened in 1796 to carry stone from the Dove Holes quarries, near Buxton, to the Peak Forest Canal at Bugsworth (known, for cosmetic reasons, as Buxworth since 1935, but possibly about to revert to the original name). The trains of the tramway were horse-drawn for much of the route, but a gravitation railway was used for the steepest section between Top o'th'Plain and Chapel. In the 1880s, up to 600 tons of lime a day was being loaded into barges which carried their cargo along the Peak Forest Canal to Manchester and beyond. The tramway closed in 1926 and the track was removed in 1936. The route of the tramway is still clearly visible in many areas and some of the stone blocks which carried the tracks are still on the ground.

73 The High Peak Laundry was located in Barmoor Clough. Its advertisements were highly evocative: 'The laundry is situated in the Peak of Derbyshire, and stands at an altitude of something like 1,200 ft above sea level. The air in the district is beautifully sweet and pure, eminent medical men having declared it to be unequalled in the country. The water is obtained from several well-known springs, including the famous Ebbing and Flowing Well, one of the Seven Wonders of the Peak. Whenever possible, all clothes are grass bleached and dried in the open air. The advantages of this laundry will be obvious. The clothes sent out possess that delightfully sweet smell which is always associated with country drying. The linen is of the purest white, and from a health point of view, there is a striking contrast between this and the ill-ventilated and unhealthy laundries of large towns'.

74   Sparrowpit is described by Humphrey Pakington in 'English Villages and Hamlets' as 'a mere handful of grey houses and which has a certain picturesqueness as it stands stolidly facing the winds of heaven'. The village is a high-level, linear settlement with almost all the houses on one side of the street. The origin of the place-name is uncertain. Sparrowpit possibly derives from Spar Row, the row of miners' cottages which make up the bulk of the village, but seventeenth century records contain a reference to Sparrowpitte Yatte. Yatte is an old English word meaning a pass in a hilly district or boundary point. There are old lead workings to the north and east of the village, some of which are planted with trees, in the Derbyshire manner, to prevent cattle from grazing on lead-polluted land. Tin miners from Cornwall are said to have moved into the area to work the lead rakes.

75   Sparrowpit's village road drops down from its highest point at Peaslows to the Wanted Inn at the crossroads. The inn was given its name when it was bought by Mr. and Mrs. Buswell after a two-year period when it had been empty and unwanted. The Buswells have another claim to fame: their son is the actor who played Ray Langton in 'Coronation Street'. The Wanted Inn was known previously as the Devonshire Arms and was but one of three inns in the village. Sparrowpit was one of the earliest Methodist communities in the country: a Methodist church was established here in 1738. The present church, which was built in the nineteenth century, has a cellar which used to house the village blacksmiths. Some houses have wells in their cellars.

76 We end with this superb view of the High Peak landscape north of Chapel-en-le-Frith. The town of Chapel has never had a picture postcard prettiness: its buildings are sturdy, rather than picturesque. But, as we have seen, Chapel has a long history, a splendid Old Town and many fascinating monuments. Chapel-en-le-Frith has suffered some physical neglect over recent years, but a newly re-formed Regeneration Partnership, involving Parish, Borough, and County Councils, local traders and the Amenity Society, offers the hope of a sensitive renovation of the old Capital of the Peak.

The wonderful landscape which surrounds the town is largely unspoilt, because the gritstone hills enjoy the protection of National Park status.